AND ON THE EIGHTH DAY GOD MADE AMERICA

SIMON BOND

TOTALLY U.S.

A Methuen Paperback

A Methuen Paperback

First published in Great Britain in 1988
by Methuen London
Michelin House, 81 Fulham Road, London SW3 6RB
Copyright © Polycarp Ltd 1988

Photoset and Printed in Great Britain
by Redwood Burn Limited, Trowbridge, Wiltshire

British Library Cataloguing in Publication Data

Bond, Simon, 1947–
Totally U.S.
1. English humorous cartoons. Collections
from individual artists
I. Title
741.5'942

ISBN 0–413–17370–4

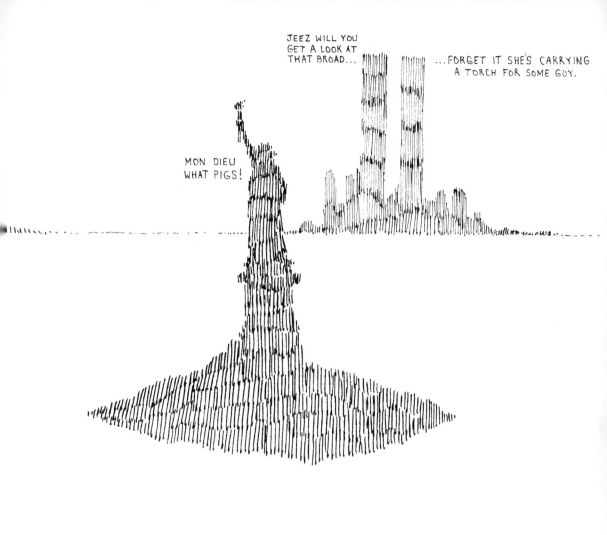

WELCOME
TO NEW YORK

PLEASE HAVE YOUR
MONEY READY

'Belwood, the market's down . . . wake me in a week.'

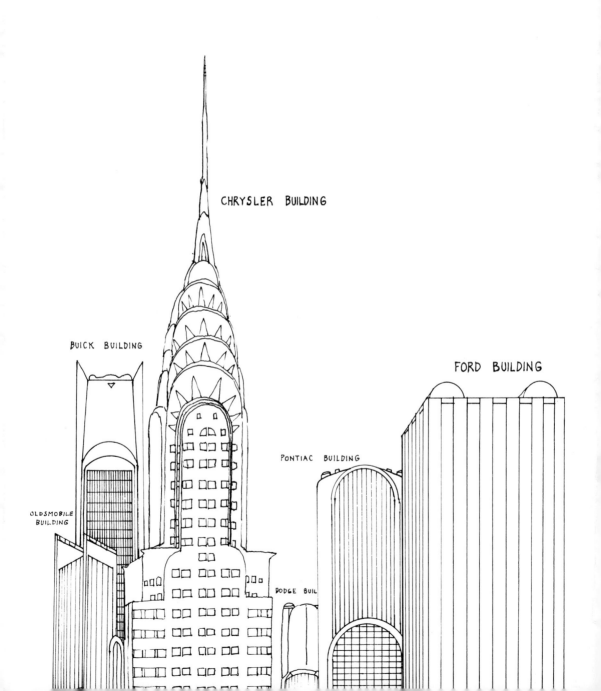

CHRYSLER BUILDING

BUICK BUILDING

FORD BUILDING

PONTIAC BUILDING

OLDSMOBILE
BUILDING

DODGE BUIL

CONEY ISLAND 1491

THE BREAKFAST MEETING
*Can you spot the deliberate mistake?

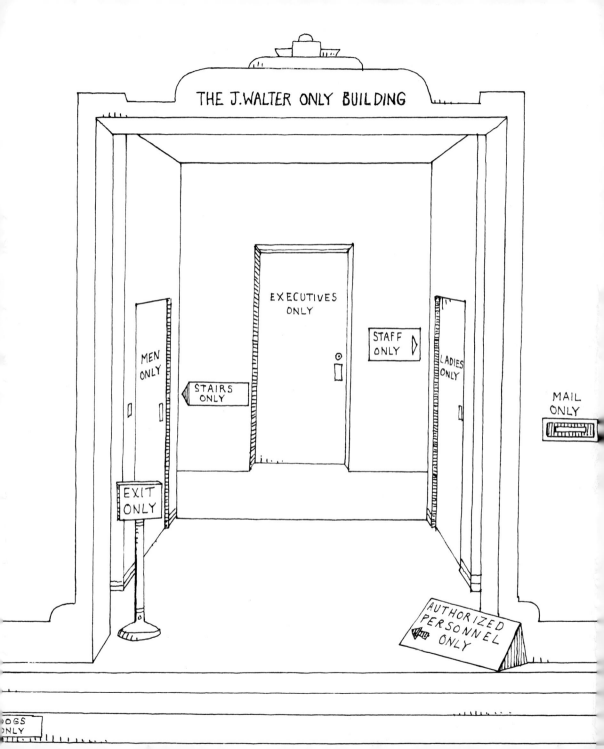

GUCCI

SEARS

BROOKS BROS.

THE WOMENS WEAR DAILY MAP OF AMERICA

THE JUSTIFIED DEATH OF A SALESMAN

THE PRESIDENT
EATS OUT

'One burger and eight fries to go.'

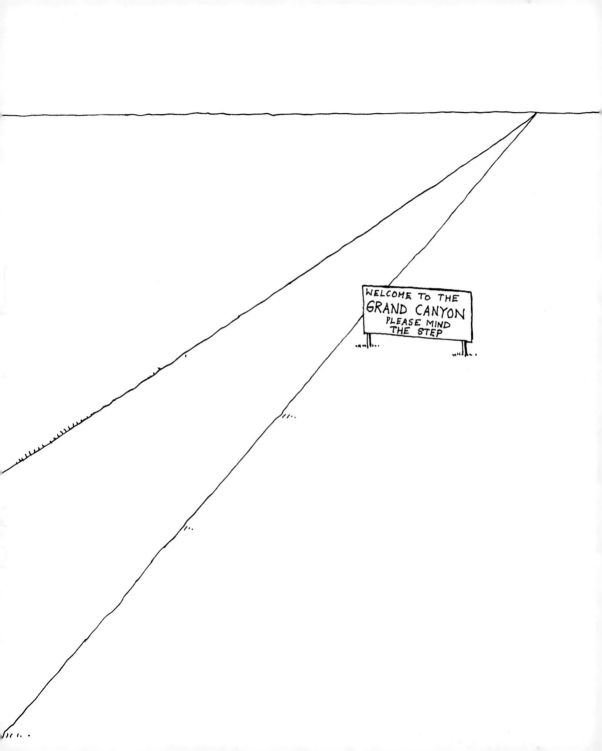

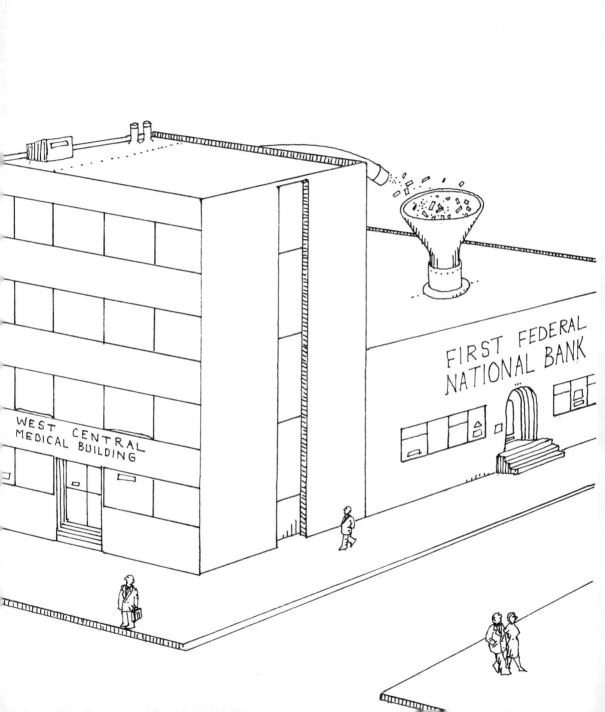

KENNEDY AIRPORT

PLANES DEPARTING	PLANES ARRIVING	PLANES PASSING BY	PLANES NOWHERE NEAR HERE
PA 109 LONDON	TWA 10 PARIS	A. MEXICO 70 MEXICO C.	AERO ACME DUBLIN
BA 64 M'CHESTER	AIR FR. 792 PARIS	AEROFLOT 88 WARSAW	ACE AIR 99 PHX. AZ.
TWA 171 ROME	SAB 10M BRUSSELS	B. CAL 680 GLASGOW	WIZZO AIR 6 NEWARK N.J.
PA 400 MADRID	EL AL 266 TEL AVIV	EASTERN 18 DALLAS	EL TORRO 60 S. DIEGO
LUF. 800 BERLIN	BA 68 BAHRAIN	WEST 604 SAN. FRAN	CROPDUST 16 KANSAS
	AIR CANADA LONDON		

'Eight guilty, three not guilty
and one peperoni pizza with extra cheese.'

'I'll be a little late home honey . . . I'm meeting with my lawyers!'

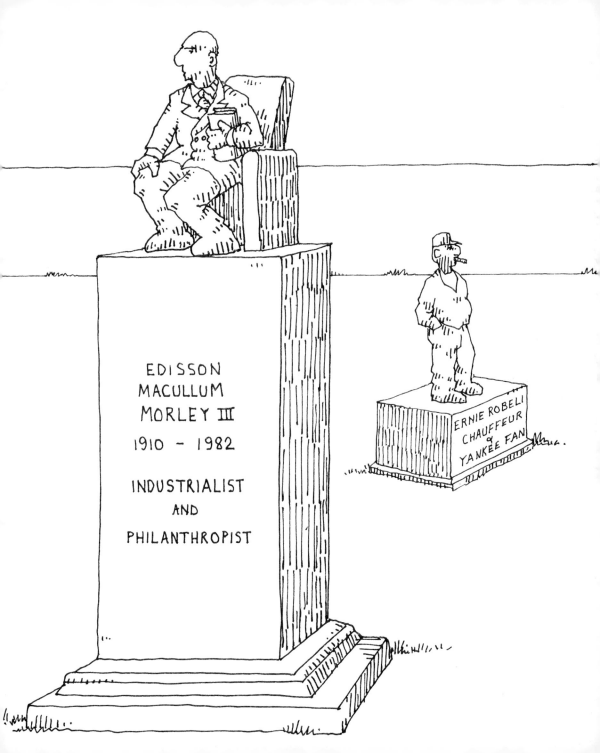

EDISSON
MACULLUM
MORLEY III

1910 – 1982

INDUSTRIALIST
AND
PHILANTHROPIST

ERNIE ROBELI
CHAUFFEUR
&
YANKEE FAN

HEAVY—HANDED SATIRE

MARTHA'S VINEYARD

MARTHA'S DRUNK

WHY WE HAVE ARCHITECTS

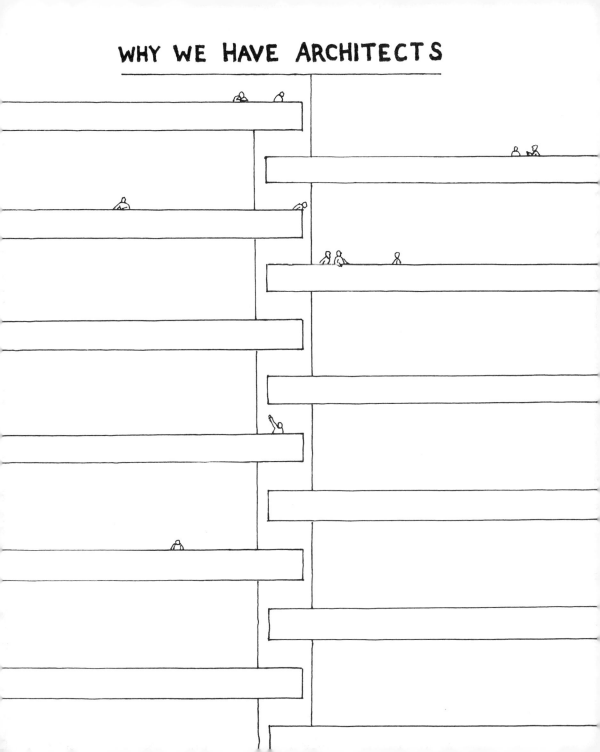

THE STATE OF THE NATION

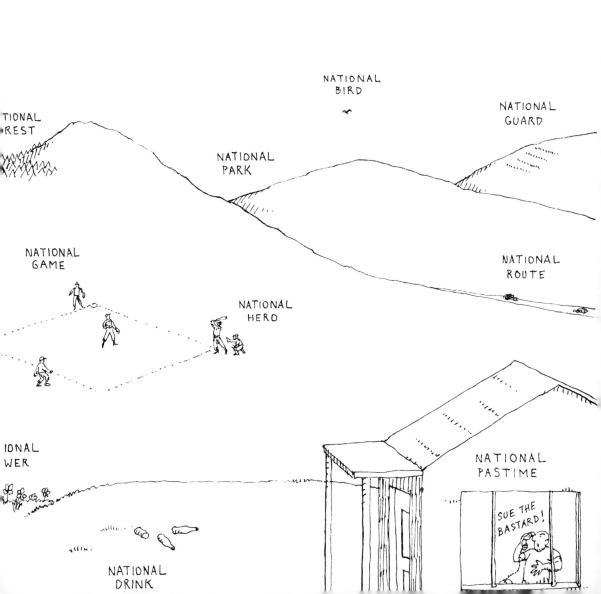

NATIONAL
BIRD

NATIONAL
GUARD

TIONAL
REST

NATIONAL
PARK

NATIONAL
GAME

NATIONAL
HERO

NATIONAL
ROUTE

IONAL
WER

NATIONAL
PASTIME

SUE THE
BASTARD!

NATIONAL
DRINK

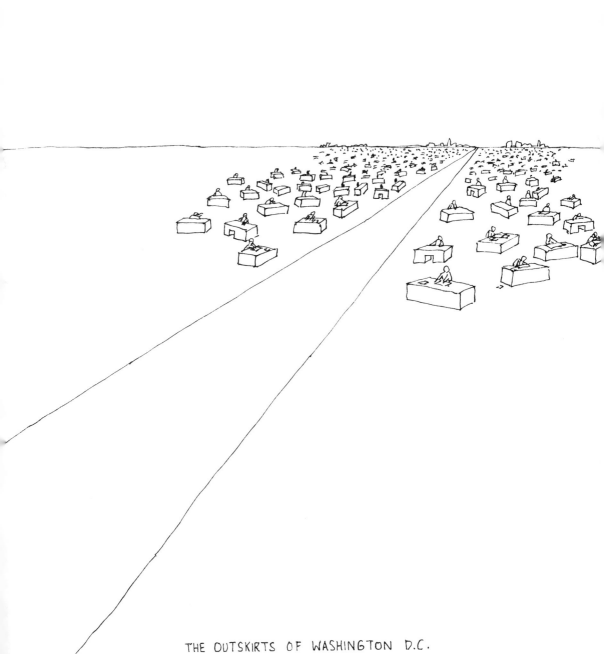

THE OUTSKIRTS OF WASHINGTON D.C.

WELCOME TO
SEQUEETA
COUNTY

ALL WELCOME

EXCEPT
BLACKS
JEWS
COMMIES
HIPPIES
MEXICANS
YANKIES

AND
LIBERALS
LIBBERS
CATHOLICS
OR
HOMOS

PLUS ANYONE
WITH A THREE
FIGURE I.Q.

BEAVERVILLE
MONTANA
POP 67 EST 1865

'. . . and then you take a left at the First Church of Christ the Redeemer . . . another left at the Everlasting Baptist Chapel . . . second right at the Neverending Chapel of God the Giver . . . straight past the Holy House of God the Good . . . another right at the Trinity Church of the Secular Servant . . . left at the Metro Miracle Mid-Town Tabernacle . . .'

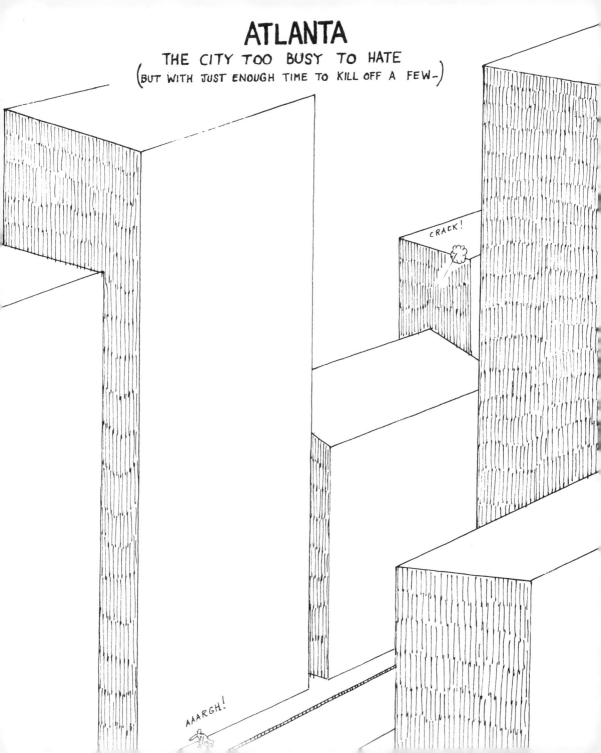

A NEW CASH CROP FOR ALABAMA

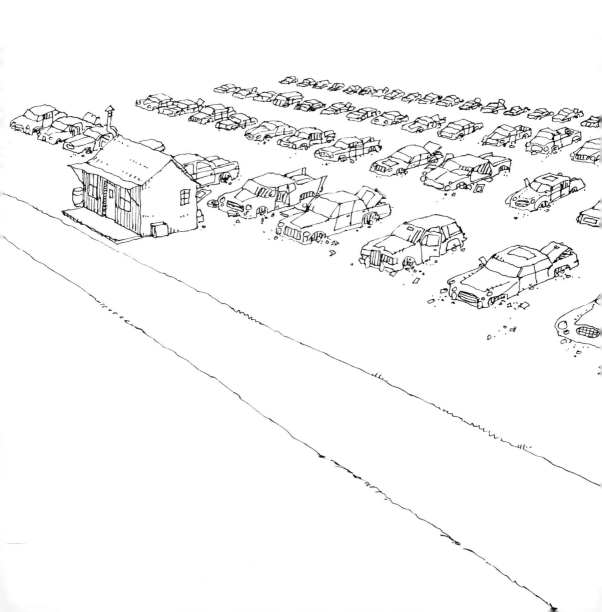

DIVORCE COURT

'It's rather a crude system but the customers seem to like it.'

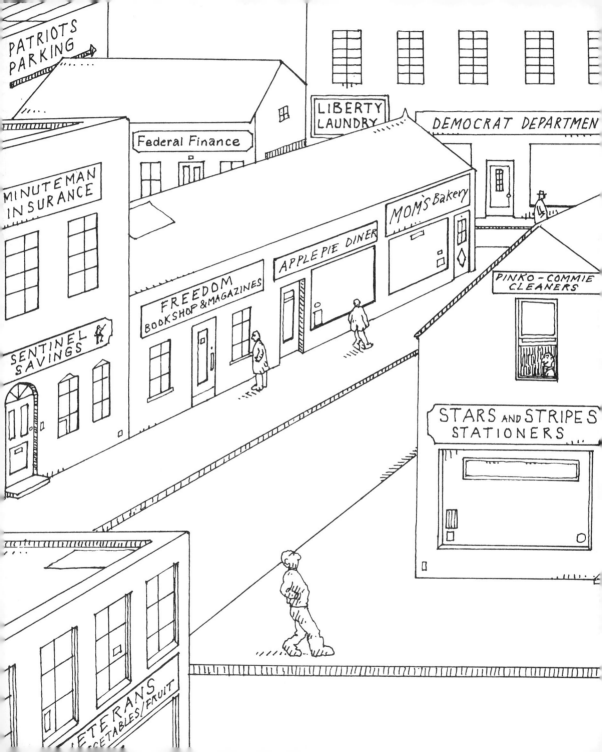

'I'd like to buy a book on chutzpah
and I'd like you to pay for it.'

'I loved the book and the mini-series,
but I wasn't so keen on the record or the movie,
although the stage version and video were okay.'

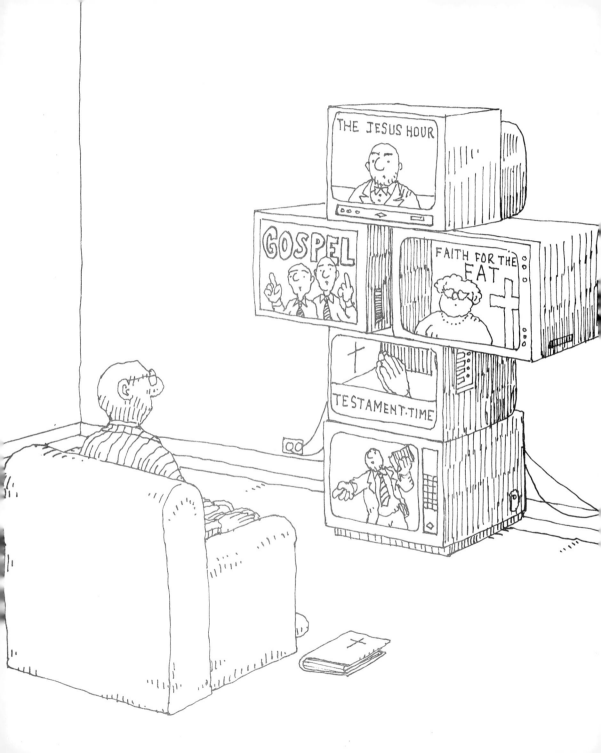

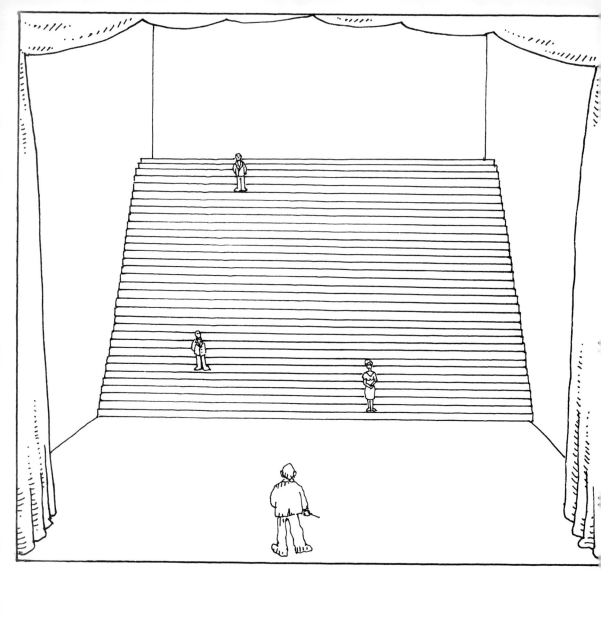

THE MORMON TABERNACLE TRIO

A CONGRESSIONAL HEARING

SUNDAY IN THE PARK

'Apparently I'm from New Heidelberg Springs, South Dakota . . .
but just where the hell is that?'

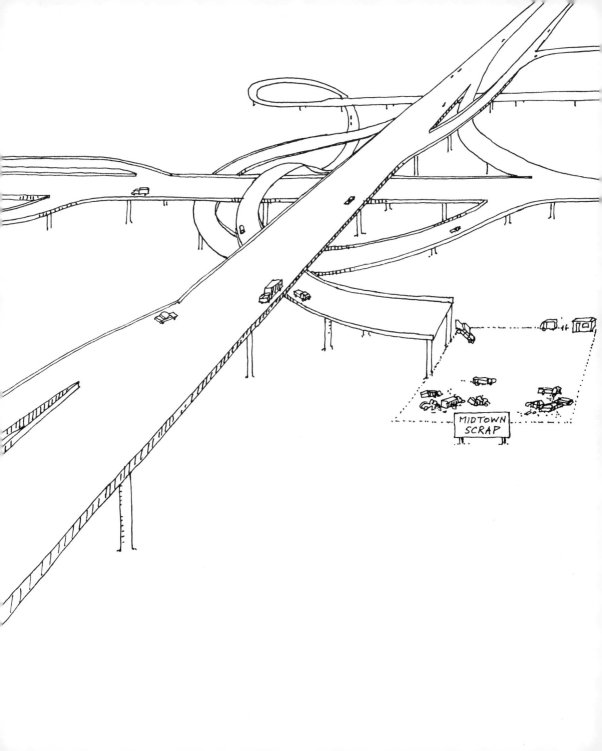

THE CONVERSATION FLAGGED
AFTER DELWOOD DIED

GOD BLESS AMERICA

THE LAND OF THE FREE & HOME OF THE BRAVE

'More tea, dear?'

'Oh my God, the Apache Nation Marching Band!'

NEWTOWN FALLS
NEW HAMPSHIRE
POP. 204
REPUBLICAN 8
DEMOCRAT 2
NONE OF YOUR DAMN BUSINESS 194

A CORRIDOR OF POWER

WASHINGTON D.C.

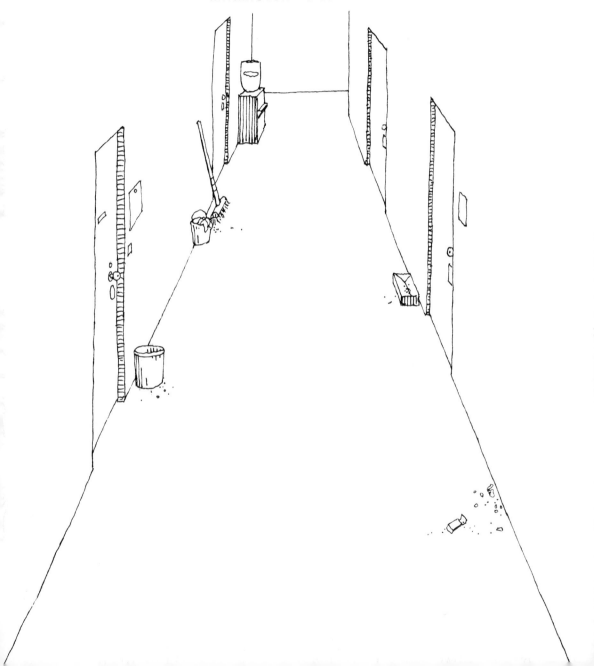

UNEXPECTED AMERICANS—*The Liberal Trucker.*

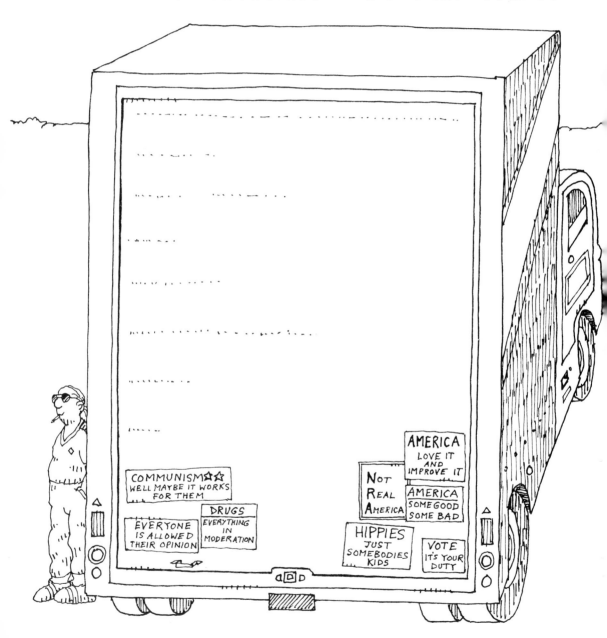

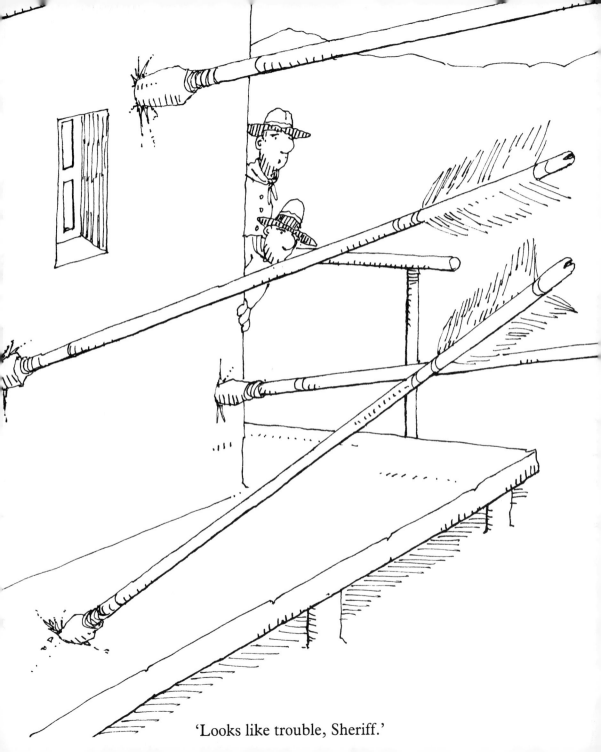

'Looks like trouble, Sheriff.'

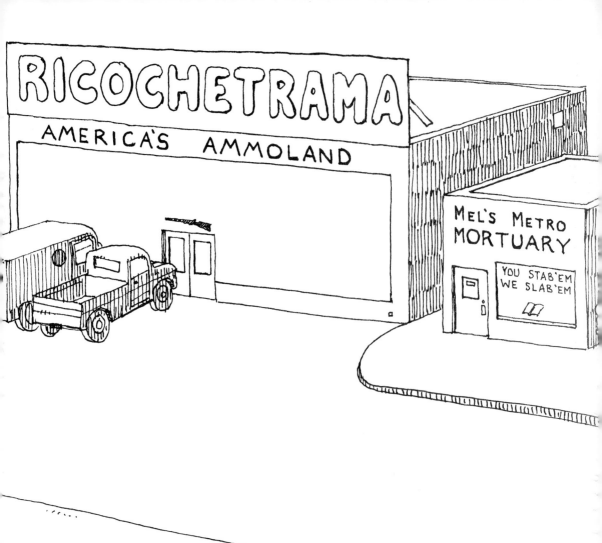

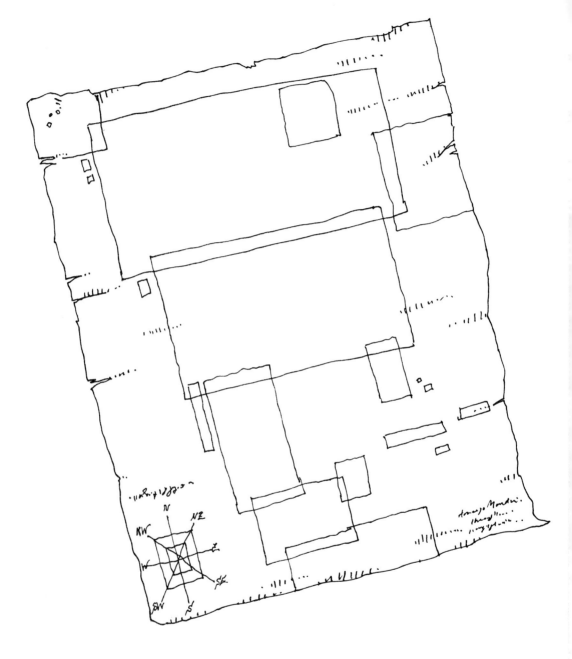

Amerigo Mondrian Discovers America 1491

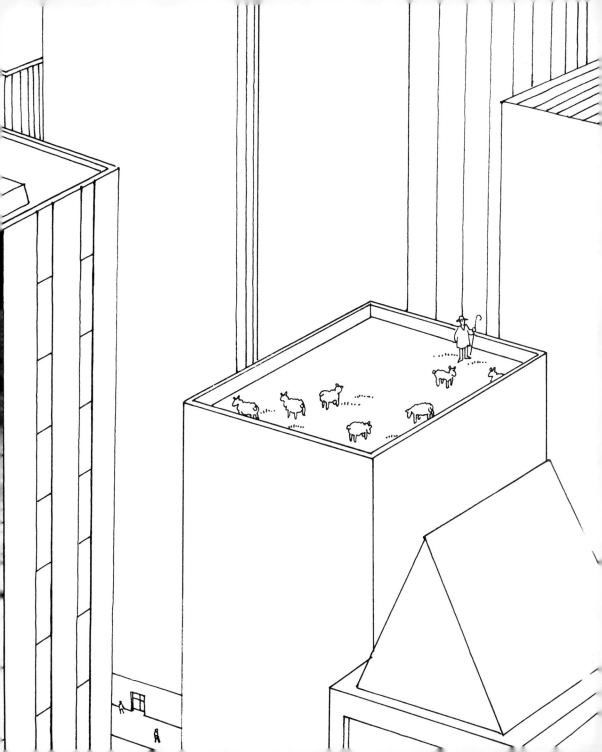

DIPLOMACY IN ACTION

'Listen buddy, you'd better become a Democracy by Thursday
or we'll bomb the shit out of you!'

THE CINCINNATI BENGALS FORMATION DANCE TEAM

'I love it . . . but lose the bodies.'

'Thank you Lord for everything and by the way there's no more
tax on any of this is there?'

◯ JUPITER

◯ VENUS

◯ MARS

EARTH

CALIFORNIA

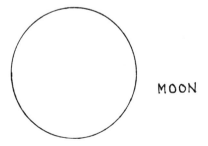

MOON

'It's all right . . . there's a lot of them,
but they've all surrendered.'

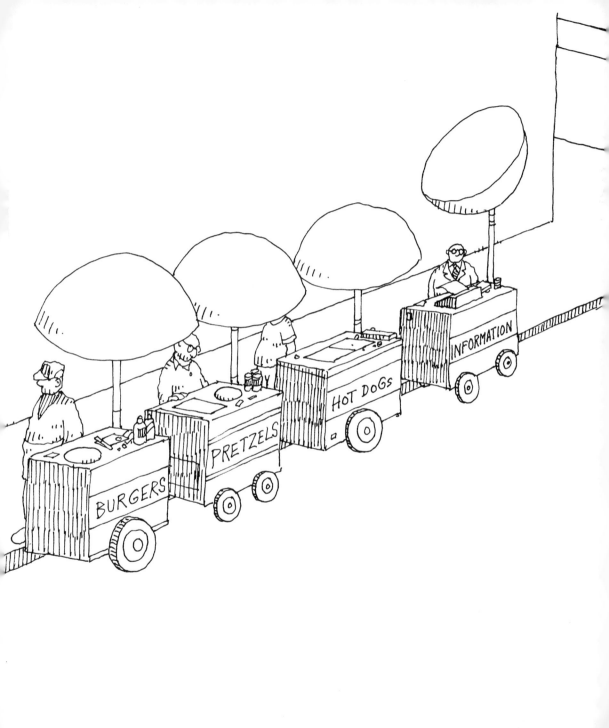

Hallo, I'm Jeff... I'm your customer today...
we'd both like mineral water to start and a menu
My particular special is coq au vin and we will
not be needing a wine list. We certainly hope
to enjoy our meal and should we need
anything, we'll certainly let you know.

PENNY CANDY
BOTTLED MILK
THE BROOKLYN DODGERS
RIP
HOWDY DOODY
STUDEBAKER
BURMA SHAVE
5¢ CIGAR

FINALLY AN HONEST MAN

'. . . and I promise to lie and cheat and line my pockets at each
and every opportunity.'

'Oh well, it'll have to do.'